Santa's Dashboard

Written and Illustrated by

Jerome Connelly Farmer

Santa's Dashboard
Text and Illustrations Copyright © 2014 by Jerome Connelly Farmer
All rights reserved.
Love and Learn Books
Del Mar, CA

Farmer, Jerome Connelly
Santa's Dashboard / Text and illustrations by Jerome Connelly Farmer
"Love and Learn Books."
Summary: A young boy takes Santa's sleigh in order to escape from bullies
and rescue his puppy, but fears he will be in trouble if Santa catches him.
ISBN 978-0-692-33833-9
[1. Christmas – Fiction. 2. Santa Claus – Fiction. 3. Technology – Fiction.]
First Edition

For my parents,
Carolyn and Jerome,
who taught me the meaning
of unconditional love.

We had no where to go and had walked for blocks,
But I got an idea when I found a box.
So I walked to the steps of a house that was near.
It was a good plan, even if I had a tear.

"Look, Ruffy, this will be your new home," I said.
"At least one of us will have food and a bed.
They'll want to keep you when they see my note."
So, I put him in a box. This is what I wrote:

> This present will love you, from his head to his paws.
> He'll make your home perfect, I promise!
> —Love, Santa Claus

I started to leave, but then heard a noise.
To my great alarm, it was the mean boys.

I opened the box and yelled, "Run, Ruffy, run!"
If these boys caught us, it would not be fun.

Those big kids were fast. I could not get away.
All I could do was to think, hope, and pray.
I jumped on some vines and tried to climb high,
But the meanest kid chased me as I went towards the sky.

The sight I beheld made me want to cheer –
For on top of the roof, were nine mighty reindeer!

They were friendly to me.
 Their eyes sparkled with laughter.
But Rudolph snarled at the boy who climbed up after.

Santa's sleigh had a smell, like a heavenly treat.
I searched and found cookies from Mrs. Claus on the seat.
I couldn't resist — I ate Santa's snack,
But I almost got caught and had to jump in a sack.

Inside of the bag it was darker than night.
I opened a present and found a flashlight.
The next box surprised me with lots of food.
"The bag knows what I need!" I thought as I chewed.

After a while, I decided to peek.
I liked the view from so high and the wind on my cheek.
I saw wonderful, fabulous sights as we soared,
But nothing as amazing as Santa's dashboard.

The dashboard was sparkling with gadgets galore,
It had all sorts of things you can't buy in a store.
There was nothing for speed and nothing to steer,
But switches for laughter and throttles for cheer.
There was a button for joy and a dial for glow,
And to prepare for landing, Santa turned a knob to add snow.

Santa pressed '`Enlarge Chimney`.' Then he walked away.
So I said, "Show me Ruffy," to the dashboard display.
And there he appeared – my dog on the screen.
He was running away from those boys who were mean.

"Noooo, Ruffy!" I yelled, "Please do not jump!"
But he did, and my throat filled with a lump.
I was scared, but instead of reacting to fright,
I turned the 'Slow Time' knob all the way right.

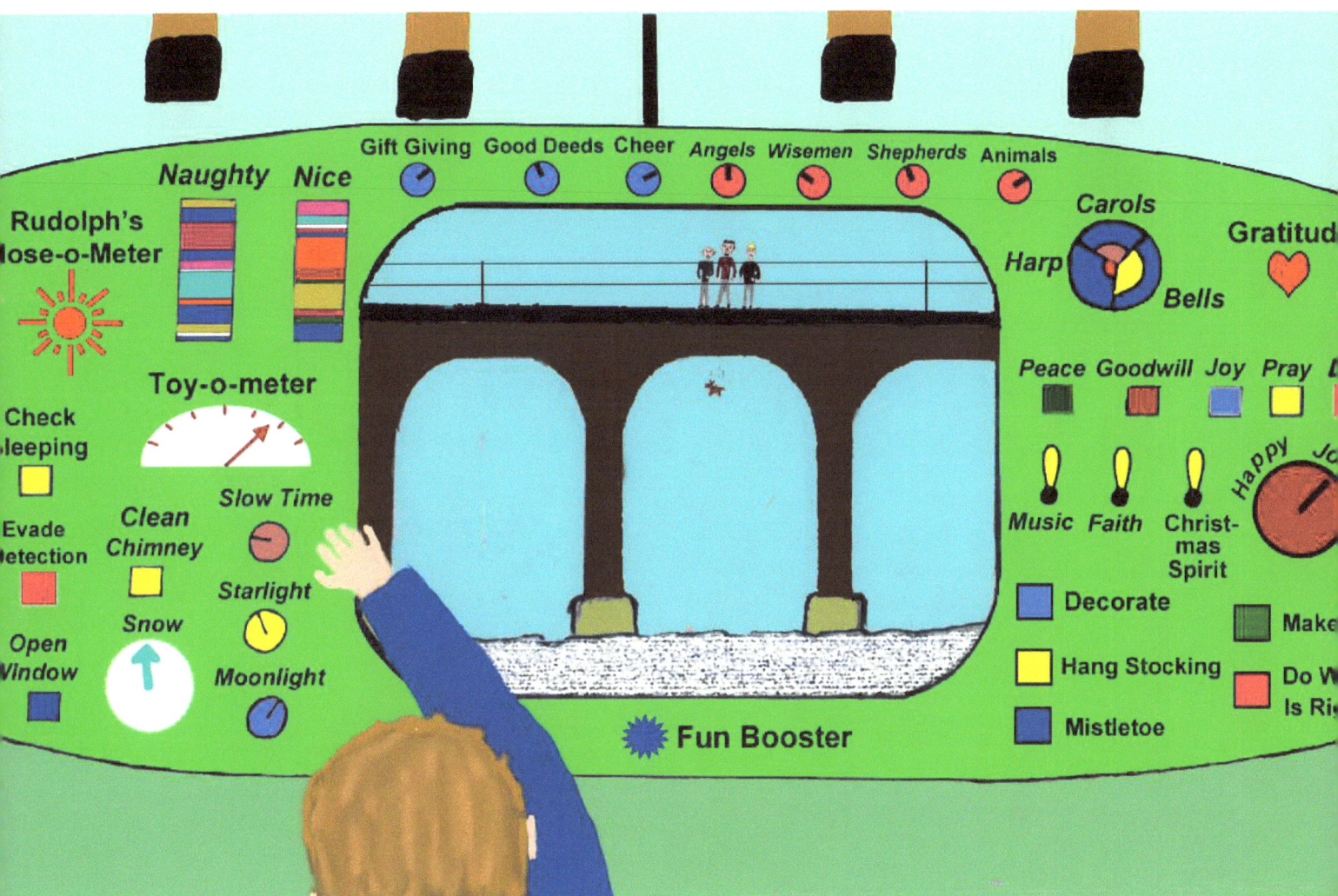

Grabbing the reins, I yelled, "To Ruffy! Let's go!"
We shot up like a rocket with extra turbo.
Between cities and counties the reindeer dashed.
At least ten thousand times, we nearly crashed.

I couldn't slow down and there was no brake.
I tried buttons and switches — that was a mistake.
Windows and chimneys formed in the wrong places.
Presents were gone. I imagined sad faces.
I would be disliked by every kid and adult.
Christmas was ruined and it was my fault.

Then suddenly I saw a button named 'Peace.'
I pushed it, expecting the chaos to cease.
I decided, "Why don't I loosen the reins?"
And then we were flying as smooth as airplanes.
Can you imagine my awesome delight,
As I piloted reindeer in well-controlled flight?

"To Ruffy," I yelled as the sleigh started to climb,
Then I pressed a button labeled 'Make It In Time.'
The reindeer were at the bridge in a snap.
I stopped under Ruffy. He fell in my lap.

Then the mean boy above threw a rock at the sleigh.
You must admit, that's not a nice way to play.
So I aimed at his face and pressed 'Open Window.'
His mouth got big fast, and continued to grow.
But he kept saying bad words as he was talking.
So, I aimed at his tongue and pressed 'Hang Stocking.'

"Ruffy," I said, "My next idea is great!"
Then I aimed at all three boys and pressed 'Decorate.'

"We can't go back, Ruffy, but we can have a blast!"
So, we zoomed around the world, going super fast...

In Manila, we saw star lanterns made from bamboo.

"These are Christmas traditions," I said as we flew.

In Sweden, a giant straw goat was burned.

In Estonia, people went to a sauna, we learned.

Christmas was happy all over, we saw on our search.
In Caracas, they even roller skated to church!

Then I saw a button labeled 'Do What is Right.'
I pressed it, and turned sharp in the night.
Back to Santa we headed, to return the sleigh,
For perhaps there was a chance he could save Christmas Day.
But, we couldn't get caught – no that wouldn't do.
So I put Ruffy in a bag and I jumped in too.

The first present was food; a truck worked like a plate.
I told Ruffy my plan, as my hungry dog ate:
"Every time Santa goes down a family's chimney,
I'll peek out of the bag and check what I see.
At the right house — the best there can be —
I'll leave you in a box, under the tree.
I'll make sure you're happy, with kids who like to play.
Once you have a home, I'll run far away."

It took lots of work, but I found the right place. I set out the box, and I watched just in case.

"No, Ruffy!" I whispered, "Stay under the tree."
But my little dog just wouldn't listen to me.
He popped out his head and jumped over a track.
Then he ran back to me and leaped into the sack.

This time I sealed the box up so tight.
I used lots of tape and got it just right.
I wrote the same note as I had twice before,
And signed it from Santa, so they'd like Ruffy even more.

Then a big scary hand reached into the sack.
I struggled and fought, but was caught by the back!

Santa set me down where two people stood.
They smiled as if I was special and good.
Santa said, "These people have wanted a child for years."
The man looked so happy, his wife had joyful tears.

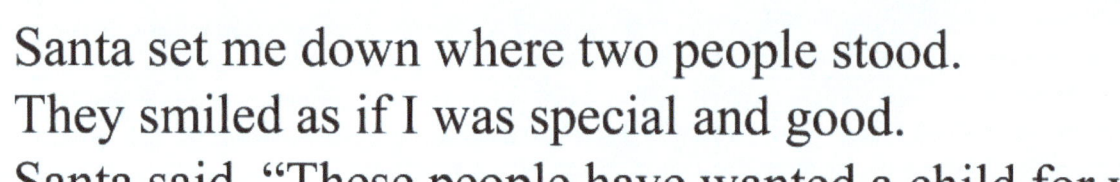

"They're on my Nice List, will you give them a chance?"
I felt small and shy, but my heart wanted to dance.
"Yes," I said fast, before this chance slipped away.
I remembered Santa's dashboard...
         when I had pressed 'Love' and 'Pray.'

I thought this was the happiest a person could be –
Then Santa handed a present to me.

Jerome Connelly Farmer is an inventor, engineer, and businessman. He has three technical degrees from Stanford University and has worked in Silicon Valley, consulted at several Hollywood studios, and been involved in many start-up companies. He is a wildlife photographer and has has taken pictures in all seven continents, including Komodo dragons in Indonesia, macaws in the Amazon rain forest, endangered species in the Galapagos Islands, duck-billed platypus in Australia, and white rhinoceros in Botswana.

Jerome is a pilot, sailor and scuba diver, and has retraced parts of Ernest Shackleton's famous rescue in Antarctica. He lives in Del Mar, California.

CPSIA information can be obtained
at www.ICGtesting.com
Printed in the USA
LVHW071746101222
734968LV00013B/1034